My Olympic Story

Written by Kwame Nkrumah-Acheampong
Illustrated by Philip Bannister

Contents

Collins

Growing up

I was born in 1974 in Glasgow, but when I was one year old we moved back to Ghana. We moved around a lot when I was young, and after a year in Ghana we moved to Zambia. My dad had got a new job at the university there, and we lived on the university campus in Lusaka. Then, when I was about five, we moved again, to Nigeria and that's where I went to primary school.

Glasgow, Scotland

2

When I was 13 we moved again, back to Ghana. Although I was sad because I wasn't going to see some of my friends again, coming back to Ghana was extremely exciting. We got in the car and drove all the way.

I was the new kid in school again and because I spoke differently from all the other children, it was difficult at first, but I made friends quickly, partly I think because I was so sporty. Even though I was really short and tiny, I was tough and my **muscular** structure was developed, so I could run faster and jump higher than bigger kids. I joined lots of school teams and made friends that way.

me, on the right, with a school friend

King of the castle

When I went to university, I got into a lot of sports. Actually, it became a bit difficult to do it all. I'd get up at about five in the morning and go training, then I'd come back, go for lectures, and after lectures I'd go training again. So, it was full on.

Lawn tennis was my favourite sport, I was number one in the university for two or three years in a row and it was nice to rule the whole castle – I loved it.

I also enjoyed **track and field**, but because I wasn't a mad runner I kind of stumbled into the track and field. I knew I could run fast and I knew I could run long, but I was always afraid that I wouldn't do well in real competitions. But when I competed against the track and field guys in training, I passed all of them, so the coach said I should join the team.

From Ghana to the UK

After university, I decided to move to the UK and continue studying there. I knew about the UK, because we'd stayed there for two or three days on the way to America when I was young, but when I arrived it was snowing and it was the first time I'd actually seen snow. I knew what it was, but it was the first time I'd experienced it.

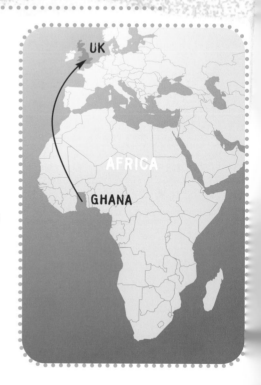

UK

AFRICA

GHANA

It was snowing when I arrived in the UK.

the snowdome, Milton Keynes

I had to work to pay for my studies, so when I saw a job advert at the **snowdome** in Milton Keynes, I sent in my CV and in October 2001 they gave me a job on reception.

9

To the slopes

About a week after I got
the job I started skiing.
I had a 30-minute lesson and
did a hockey stop without being
taught, which is when you
come to a stop by putting your
skis sideways, and that was my
first time on skis!

After that I tried to join
lessons whenever I could, and
if none of the instructors were
free I'd just go on the slope on
my own. I was in a hurry
to learn. If I had a lunch break, I'd do 30 minutes. If it was my
day off I'd do two hours. If I finished my shift, I'd ski for an hour
before I went home: an hour here, 30 minutes there. I ended up
doing more and more freestyle, jumps and things, and I didn't use
skis – I used blades. Blades are shorter than skis, so it's more
dangerous and harder than skiing, it's like being on skates on
the ski slope. Anyway it wasn't long before I became part of
the freestyle scene at the snowdome.

Onwards and upwards

Because I was skiing so much and getting pretty good, one of the instructors suggested that I try out my skiing on a real mountain and if possible, compete in some races.

the Alps in France, where I first skied on a real mountain

So I signed up for an event in France to test how well I could ski on a mountain. It was nerve-wracking because there was so much pressure: there were three camera crews filming, a **potential sponsor** was there to watch me, promising me a **sponsorship** deal if I could make it down, and they'd given me extremely long skis when I'd been used to short skis. If I could ski from the top of the mountain down to the bottom without falling down, I stood a chance. So I decided to just go in a straight line, not to try to turn because I knew that if I fell, it was game over. It was frightening to go that fast but it felt great to get to the bottom.

13

I survived the test and a company called me and offered me a season pass. That was my first sponsorship, but it wasn't much. It was up to me to find my equipment and everything else. I didn't have a clue how I was going to do it. I just knew that if I was prepared to fight hard, maybe I could **qualify** for the Turin Winter Olympic Games in 2006, so I quit my job and stayed in France for the winter season.

To qualify I had to get a lot better, and France is one of
the best places to train. Everyone thought I was crazy.
I just told them that I'd try hard to make it work, and I did.

My first ski season

I skied for most of the day, every day. I was good technically, but scared stiff of going fast, of not knowing what was on the other side of the hill. So I joined an instructors' course, not for a coaching qualification, but to study with them. I'd watch what the good guys were doing and listen to what the instructors were saying. I couldn't understand French very well, but if there was something good about one racer, I copied it.

I stayed in Meribel while I took the instructors' course. It became my home during my early training in the mountains.

After two months, I went to my first proper race. I was terrified waiting in the start gate because the slope was very different from what I'd been training on – it was an ice sheet. I just kept thinking, "Don't fall, don't do anything fantastic, it's just a matter of getting down." I made it down and everybody cheered because I don't think they expected me to do it.

There were 111 people racing, but 43 crashed and didn't finish the race. I managed to finish, but seeing so many people crash had given me this terrible fear which stayed with me for a long time. I was scared stiff, and being scared made me fall, so for the rest of the season I just fell and fell and fell. I knew that if I gave up with each fall, I'd never make it, so I'd just get up and keep going.

By the end of the ski season, I'd lost a lot of weight and was pleased to go home.

I only had one more year to try to qualify for the Turin Olympics. I felt a bit stuck because the ski season was over and while a lot of skiers train for the best part of the year, I had to come back to the UK and work over the summer. Every time I came back, I'd have to find a temporary job and work as much as I could, to make money to go out for the next season, because I couldn't rely on sponsorship.

Finally I got another deal. So, in December 2005 I headed off to Italy for another season. It felt like a race against time because most of the skiers had been on the slopes since they were four or five years old, and I was trying to get to their level in two years.

So, I'd ski every day – three hours in the morning and another three in the afternoon.

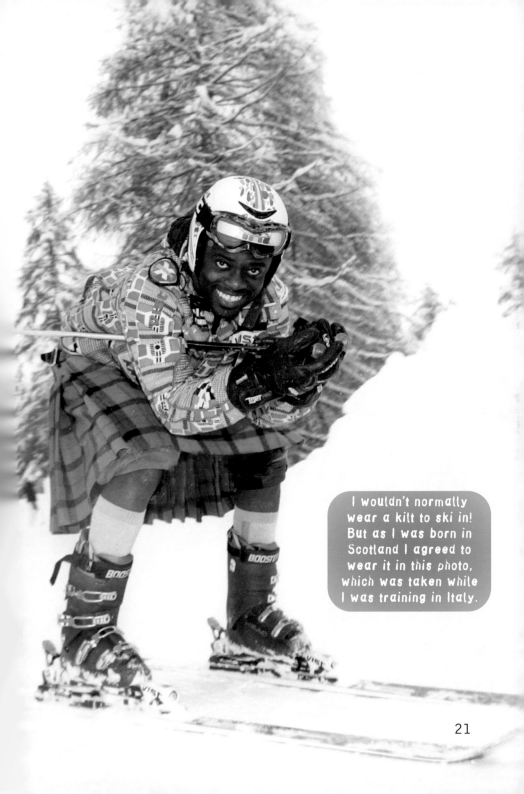

I wouldn't normally wear a kilt to ski in! But as I was born in Scotland I agreed to wear it in this photo, which was taken while I was training in Italy.

21

Disaster in Iran

As part of the qualification process for the Olympics you need to compete in a lot of races, and you can decide where to race and which ones to compete in. Because I was training in Italy, where the conditions are fantastic, and I was skiing alongside some of the best skiers in the world, I decided to do one of the races in the Middle East – in Iran. Although the conditions aren't as good and it's harder to get there, the standard of skiing is poorer, which means I could be one of the big boys.

But on my way to Iran my connecting flight was delayed, and I thought I was going to miss the flight to Iran. I got to the departure lounge and could see the plane, but was told I was too late and the doors were locked. I freaked out because I knew I had to get to Iran *that* day.

Finally they found me another flight and even though I triple checked that my baggage was checked in, when I got to Iran, nothing arrived – no baggage. So, I had to borrow somebody's skis, somebody's trousers, I didn't have my race boots, I had to wait for someone to finish racing to get their helmet and it was very messy. To wear somebody else's boots is like being **shod** with a horseshoe. It was painful and my performance wasn't as good as it should've been. I didn't qualify. It was a total waste of money and time. It felt like I'd wasted two years.

Finding future champions

I came back to the UK and didn't really know what to do,
so I started a project in Ghana to raise awareness of skiing.
Africans have a good chance at winter sports if they have
the opportunity to engage with it, so I decided to promote this sport
as much as possible and try to be the **catalyst** for something bigger.
I went to Ghana with another skier for two weeks and appeared
on the news, on TV and on the radio. We told anybody who was
interested to come along to a grass-skiing competition that we were
holding, where the winners would get to come out to Italy with me
for the next season. Lots of people turned up, but they found
it very hard, especially the balance, and one after another they
dropped out.

My ultimate dream is to see a Ghanaian on the **podium** at the Winter Olympics. The only way to achieve that is to get people interested and show them that it's possible. When I started skiing everyone told me I wouldn't be able to do it, that I'd quit – but look at me now! I think if Ghanaians start younger and can have ten years to ski, train and become good, they stand a chance of fighting for a medal.

Frozen feet at -32°C

In 2007 I competed in the World Ski Championships. It was
one of the worst ski experiences I've ever had. I'd sharpened
my skis badly and it was also the first time I'd experienced
a water-injected ski slope. When you're skiing in sub-zero
conditions, a machine injects water into the slope, turning it
into ice. It was -32°C. I don't do well in -32°C. I can cope with
-10°C, even -16°C, but not -32°C. I was extremely cold, my feet
especially, and if I can't feel my feet I can't ski, because I need
to feel the skis. I was in pain and the whole experience was bad:
the cameras, the pressure – I just panicked.

I didn't fall. I try not to fall in big competitions, I just stick
it out. But it was horrible.

I finished the World Championships in February 2008, and carried on skiing until the end of March. Then I went back to Iran, to race and try to qualify for the 2010 Olympics in Vancouver. I didn't want to wait till the next winter season to qualify.

Qualifying for the Olympics

This time everything was with me. I had my boots in the plane, just in case, because boots are the most **essential** thing. If everything goes wrong and you have your boots, you'll be OK.

Everything went very well. I qualified on the third day. It felt amazing – all the fear and stress just disappeared. I believe that I have great qualities in me: if I'm dead serious and I dig deep and push hard I'll make it. It was such a relief that all the **expenditure** had been worth it. I knew that if I hadn't qualified I would have been in a really bad place financially.

So I came home – very happy – to work and train for
the 2010 Olympics.

I hadn't yet got all of my sponsorship deals, which made it hard to train the way I wanted to train. I didn't want to spend the whole summer trying to find a sponsor, I wanted to be in France or Austria training on a **glacier**. While I waited on deals I worked out in the gym and used the indoor snow slopes, and by the time the sponsorship finally came through I only had a few weeks to prepare for the Olympics.

me with my coach

I had 22 days to train, so took to the slopes, morning, afternoon, morning, afternoon. I needed a bit of an advantage so I hit the weights, trying to get fit and strong, so when I got on the slope I wouldn't feel tired. I knew my skill wouldn't carry me all the way, but strength would carry me some of the way.

Training for the Olympics: the blue pole is called a "gate", and if you don't ski round it the right way, you get thrown out of the competition!

33

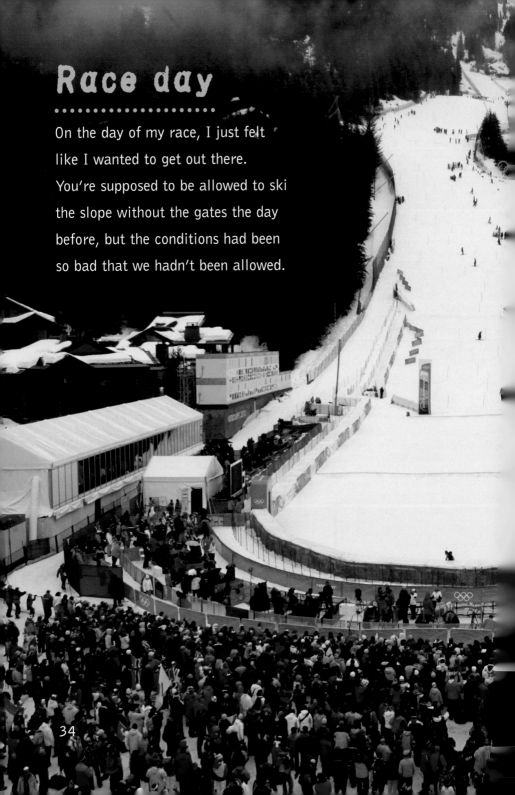

Race day

On the day of my race, I just felt
like I wanted to get out there.
You're supposed to be allowed to ski
the slope without the gates the day
before, but the conditions had been
so bad that we hadn't been allowed.

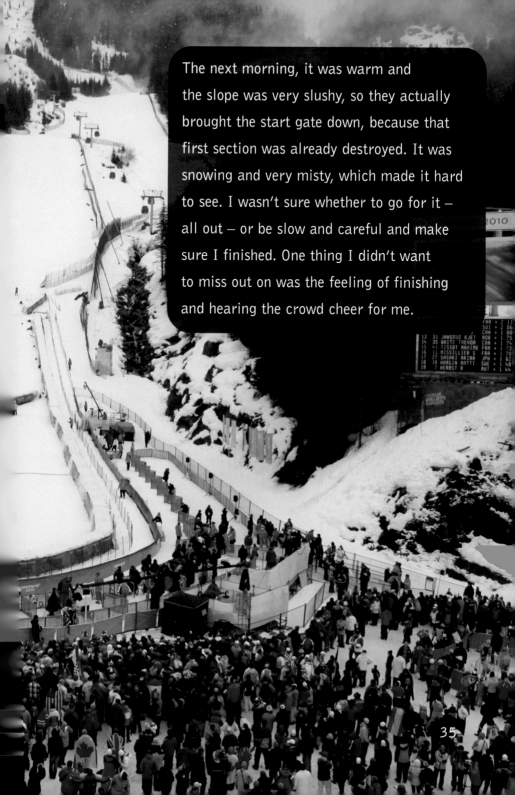

The next morning, it was warm and the slope was very slushy, so they actually brought the start gate down, because that first section was already destroyed. It was snowing and very misty, which made it hard to see. I wasn't sure whether to go for it – all out – or be slow and careful and make sure I finished. One thing I didn't want to miss out on was the feeling of finishing and hearing the crowd cheer for me.

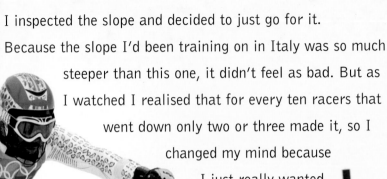

I inspected the slope and decided to just go for it.
Because the slope I'd been training on in Italy was so much
steeper than this one, it didn't feel as bad. But as
I watched I realised that for every ten racers that
went down only two or three made it, so I
changed my mind because
I just really wanted
to finish.

Waiting at the top was
very intense. I just kept
thinking: "This is it,
the whole five or six
years comes down to just
two runs. If I muck it up there's no one to blame other than
myself, because the slope is the same for everyone." I didn't
feel like I was skiing just for me any more. I had over 5,000
fans on a **social networking site**, and the whole night before
I was getting messages encouraging and supporting me
which was very nice, but also added a lot of pressure.

36

I knew my family was all there and when it was my turn the roar that came from the bottom of the slope could be heard at the top. The first run was about getting down safely, so I did that, counting each gate. I nearly fell down and heard the scream from the crowd. When I got closer to the end, I had to block out the crowd because the noise was too much, and so I just thought about each gate, because you tend to fall when you take your mind off the gates. I got down, and the crowd exploded. People were standing and screaming.

I had to do about 20 interviews before I was allowed back up
to the top, and that's when someone told me I'd missed a gate.
I thought that was that – game over. But it was a mistake and
when they confirmed my position, I found out that I hadn't missed
a gate, and in fact had beaten one other skier. My whole aim
was not to be last, so that made me feel a lot more confident.
You always feel more confident on the second run because you have
a great feel for the slope. But I was still more hesitant than if I'd
been training because I knew I was never coming back to
an Olympics again. If I failed it was going to go down in history.
So, I skied sensibly and finished and was happy. Very, very happy.

An Olympian

Finally, I felt like I could actually call myself an Olympian.
Even when I'd qualified I didn't really feel like an Olympian, but
when crowds of people mobbed me when I went out, asking for my
autograph, I realised that it was worth something to them. I realised
that people actually see the Olympics as something really important.

My goal for the Games was to prove to people that I got there through hard work and **merit**. I wanted to make sure that people saw my country in a positive light. I didn't go to win a medal, I knew I couldn't. I went to win the hearts of people, to show them that I was going to fight every inch of the way and not come last: some other country was going to end up bottom of the table, not us. Ghana had the second largest cheer in the event during the opening ceremony after Canada, so we were happy with that!

42

As a skier, being in Vancouver, flying down the slope was the most exciting point of my career. The only time I expected to be there was when I failed to qualify for the Turin Games and I sat down and asked myself if I really wanted to go through this stress again. When I decided to go for it, I knew I was going to qualify. When my back is against the wall I'll make it happen.

Glossary

catalyst	something that makes other events happen
essential	very necessary, something you can't do without
expenditure	spending, cost
glacier	a very thick sheet of ice that moves down a mountain extremely slowly, and that doesn't melt when summer comes
merit	a quality that means you deserve to do well or you have earned your success
muscular	to do with muscles
podium	a special platform that winners stand on to receive their medals
potential	possible
qualify	become good enough to be officially allowed to do something or take part in an event
shod	fitted with shoes
snowdome	a huge building with a snow-covered ski slope inside, where people can ski all year round
social networking site	a site on the Internet where people with the same interests can leave messages
sponsor	a person or a company that offers to pay for a sportsperson's training, in return for having their name displayed
sponsorship	money which companies give to sportspeople to help them pay for training and kit
track and field	sports that involve running, jumping or throwing

Index

My Olympic story

Learning to ski at the snowdome, Milton Keynes, 2001:
"I had a 30-minute lesson and did a hockey stop without being taught..."

Racing at school in Ghana, 1992:
"I could run faster and jump higher than bigger kids."

My first ski season in France, 2004:
"I just knew that if I was prepared to fight hard, maybe I could qualify for the Games."

The 2007 World Ski Championships:
"I didn't fall. I try not to fall in big competitions, I just stick it out."

Qualifying for the Olympics, 2009:
"It felt amazing - all the fear and stress just disappeared."

Skiing at the Olympics, 2010:
"Finally, I felt like I could actually call myself an Olympian."

47

❧ Ideas for guided reading ❧

Learning objectives: explore how and why writers write, including through face to face and on line contact with authors; organise text into paragraphs to distinguish between different information; deduce characters' reasons for behaviour from actions

Interest words: catalyst, expenditure, muscular, podium, potential, qualify, shod, social networking site, sponsor, sponsorship, freestyle, technically, water-injected ski slope, glacier

Curriculum links: PE: Athletic activities (2)

Resources: writing materials

Getting started

This book can be read over two or more guided reading sessions.

- Explain to the children that you are going to read a book about an Olympic athlete. Find out what children know about the Winter Olympics, e.g. *What sort of events are in the Winter Olympics, What countries are involved?*

- Ask children to name other autobiographies they have read and ask: *What is the purpose of an autobiography?* Prompt children if necessary with suggestions, e.g. *trying to inspire others; campaigning for change; explaining something interesting.*

- Ask one of the children to read the blurb and, using the glossary, make sure that children understand the terms used.

Reading and responding

- Ask children to read to the end of Chapter 1 and ask them to list Kwame's qualities as a child.

- Ask children to read up to p16 and to list the qualities Kwame has as an adult. Ask key questions to help with their list, *What kind of adult is Kwame becoming? Are there any more words to add to his description as a child? What qualities does he need to qualify for the Olympics?*